Contents

Taylor performed songs from her album *Red* with this red microphone. *Red* was Taylor's first venture into pop music from her previous country sound, with a pop-country blend that topped the charts.

Taylor made history at the 2023 Grammy Awards, shown on the red carpet here, when she won Best Music Video for "All Too Well: The Short Film." She became the first artist to win in this category who had the sole directing credit.

In July 2020, Taylor delighted fans by announcing a surprise album—*Folklore*. In December 2020, Taylor released another surprise album, *Evermore*, just five months after *Folklore*. It was a continuation of her new indie sound—Taylor describes them as "sister albums." Here, Taylor is pictured performing a mash-up of songs from both albums at the 2021 Grammy Awards.

Here, Taylor is pictured performing songs from her seventh studio album, *Lover*, in Shanghai, China. Taylor has described this album as being "a love letter to love."

Pictured here at the 2023 iHeartRadio Music Awards, Taylor wins Song of the Year for "Anti-Hero" from her tenth studio album, *Midnights*. She also won the Innovator Award and became the first living recording artist to have seven albums reach the Top 40 of the Billboard 200 chart simultaneously.

This wax figure of Taylor is in Madame Tussauds Berlin wax museum. Taylor now has nine wax figures in Madame Tussauds museums around the world.

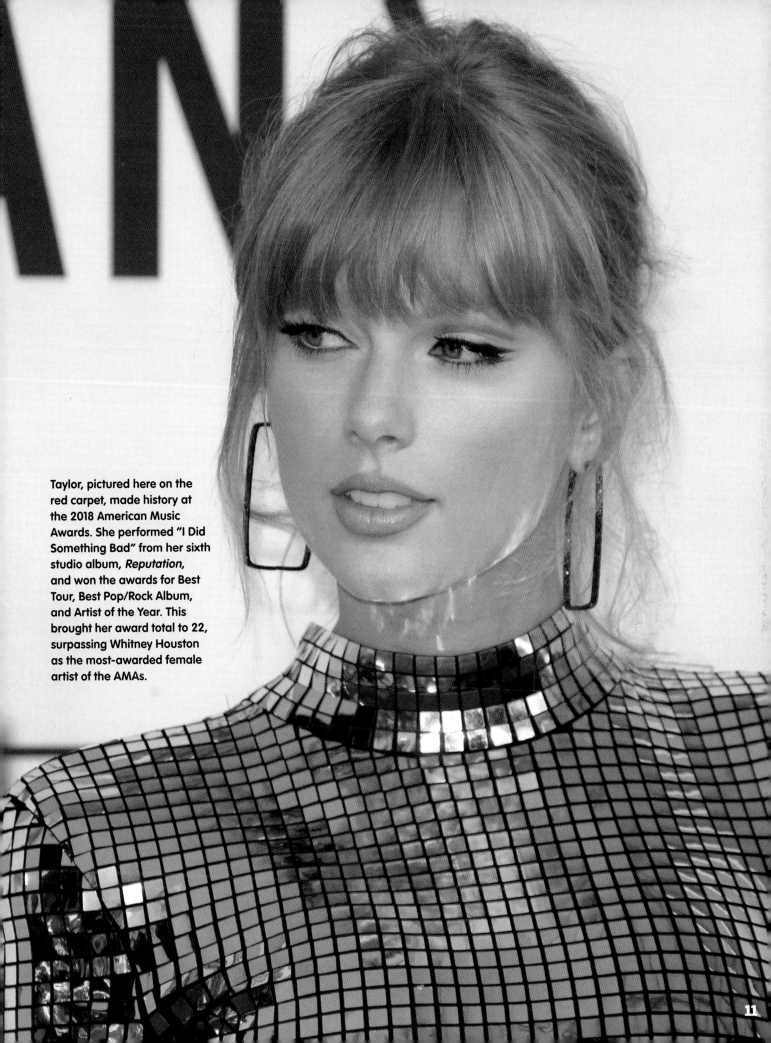

Taylor, pictured here on the red carpet, made history at the 2018 American Music Awards. She performed "I Did Something Bad" from her sixth studio album, *Reputation*, and won the awards for Best Tour, Best Pop/Rock Album, and Artist of the Year. This brought her award total to 22, surpassing Whitney Houston as the most-awarded female artist of the AMAs.

Taylor glows on the red carpet of the 2019 iHeartRadio Music Awards to accept the award for Tour of the Year for her *Reputation* tour. The tour grossed $266 million—the highest-selling tour in US history at the time. Her own record has now been surpassed—by herself! At the time of publication, Taylor's *Eras Tour* has grossed over $2.2 billion.

The guitar shown here was custom-built for Taylor. The fretboard has vines and "Taylor" written on it. Pictured is also Taylor's famous hair flip, which is one of her signature moves when playing upbeat songs.

Here, Taylor is pictured performing her song "Lover" at the 2019 iHeartRadio Jingle Ball at Madison Square Garden. Taylor wrote "Lover" aiming to create a timeless love song.

On her fifth studio album, *1989*, Taylor incorporated lots of musical styles and techniques from the decade she was born. Eighties music featured plenty of synthesizers, drum machines, and creative vocals. Pictured here, she performs at *The 1989 World Tour*.

Spot the Difference

Can you find the FIVE changes made to the image at the bottom?

Coloring

 Check off the ones you've done!

19

21

25

27

31

33

37

39

43

45

47

49

A Star is Born

Taylor Alison Swift was born on December 13, 1989, in Reading, Pennsylvania. She started playing guitar and writing songs at the age of 12, hoping to become a country singer. After years of hard work and dedication, Taylor eventually got a record deal. Her self-titled debut album, *Taylor Swift*, was released in 2006.

Feeling Lucky

Some people think the number 13 is unlucky,
but not for Taylor—it's her favorite number!
"I was born on the 13th. I turned 13 on Friday the 13th.
My first album went gold in 13 weeks . . . Basically,
whenever a 13 comes up in my life,
it's a good thing," she explained.

Country Roots

Taylor's early albums featured a lot of country music influences, which was her favorite genre as a young teenager. She would often wear cowboy boots on stage to give her outfits a country look.

The Star-Spangled Banner

In the years before her huge world tours, some of Taylor's early performances were at sports events singing the national anthem. This helped to introduce her to a new audience outside the country music scene.

Fearless

Taylor's second album, *Fearless*,
was a huge success and made her famous.
The lead single "Love Story" became
a Top 10 hit in many countries.

Fairytales

On her second album, *Fearless*, Taylor often used themes of princes and princesses, romance, and heartbreak in her lyrics and performances. The popular single "Today Was a Fairytale" was later included as a bonus track on the rerecorded *Fearless (Taylor's Version)*.

Award Winner

In 2010, Taylor won her first Grammy Awards. She picked up four awards, including Album of the Year for *Fearless*. At the time, she was the youngest person to win that award in the entire history of the Grammys.

Taylor's Guitars

Taylor has used many different guitars over the years, and sometimes plays a banjo or ukulele, too. Early in her career, being a guitarist and songwriter helped her stand out from the other aspiring country singers.

Writing Solo

After working with co-writers on her first two albums, Taylor wrote every song for *Speak Now* on her own. The record explored her growth from teenager to adulthood, and reflected on past relationships.

Share the Love

During the *Speak Now World Tour*, Taylor popularized the heart-hand gesture. "The heart-hand symbol means something between 'I love you' and 'thank you,'" she explained. "It's just a sweet, simple message that you can deliver without saying a word."

Ringleader

Taylor wore her iconic sequinned circus ringleader outfit when performing "We Are Never Ever Getting Back Together" during *The Red Tour*.

The Scarf

In the ballad "All Too Well," Taylor sings about an old scarf that an ex-boyfriend kept long after their relationship ended. Fans have speculated for years about the meaning of the scarf and who has it, but Taylor insists that it's just a metaphor!

Action!

As well as being a super-talented musician,
Taylor has appeared in several films and television
shows during her career. What's your favorite
on-screen Taylor performance?

Musical Evolution

Taylor's musical style is always evolving, which is why it's always so exciting to find out what she will do next! Over the years, she has tried her hand at country, pop, electronic, synth-pop, R&B, indie-folk, and more!

Swift Style

As her music has evolved with each album, so has Taylor's fashion. From cowboy boots and ballgowns to retro jackets, cozy cardigans, sparkly jumpsuits, and more—she never goes out of style!

A New Look

At the 2016 Met Gala, Taylor debuted a bold new look. Her hair was bleached and her makeup was more gothic, with a dark lipstick instead of her usual red. The theme of the event that year was "Fashion in an Age of Technology"—how will you style Taylor's futuristic dress?

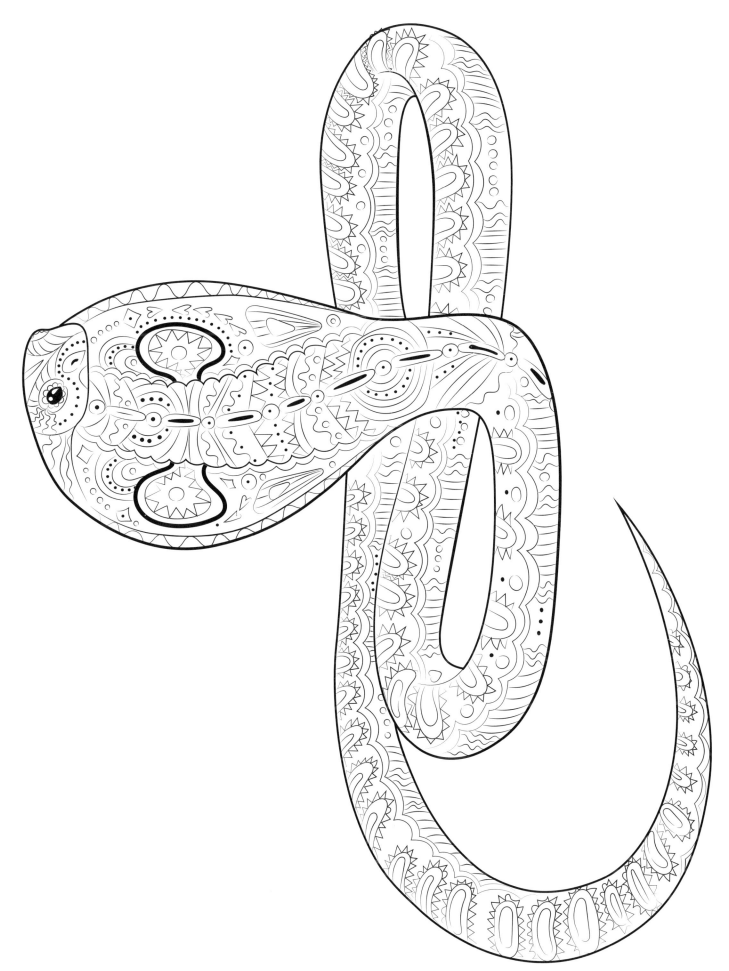

Karyn the Snake

During the *Reputation Stadium Tour*, Taylor's stage was decorated with lots of snakes, including a giant inflatable cobra called Karyn.

Giving Back

Taylor has supported many different charities and causes throughout her career. She also has a reputation for making surprise donations to fans and organizations in need.

Record Breaker

During her career so far, Taylor has repeatedly broken records for a variety of amazing accomplishments, including award wins, album sales, streaming totals, and chart successes.

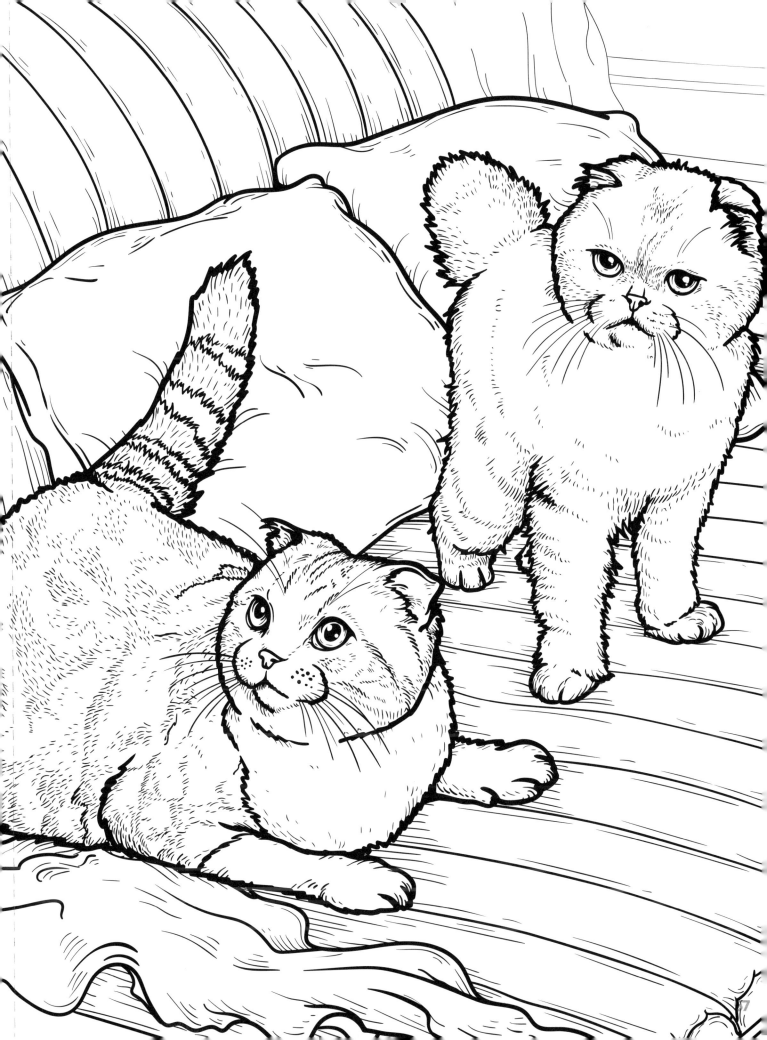

Purrrrrfect Pets

Taylor loves cats! She has adopted
two Scottish Folds—Olivia Benson and Meredith Grey,
named after her favorite TV show characters—and
a Ragdoll named Benjamin Button, named after
the literary character.

Repu-Tay-tion

Taylor's sixth album, *Reputation*, was her most personal record to date. It reflected her experiences with fame and the pressures of living in the public eye, but also explored how she fell in love amid the chaos of it all.

Activism

In recent years, Taylor has been using her fame to help raise awareness of different social and political issues. "I felt like I had to speak up to try and help make a change," she explained.

Spreading Her Wings

Taylor's seventh album, *Lover,* is filled with colorful imagery and butterfly motifs that represent her moving on and leaving the darker themes of *Reputation* behind.

Taking a Stand

When the master copies of Taylor's first six albums were purchased against her will, she decided to take action. She has been rerecording the albums, from *Taylor Swift* to *Reputation*, and releasing new "Taylor's Version" editions, which she owns the rights to.

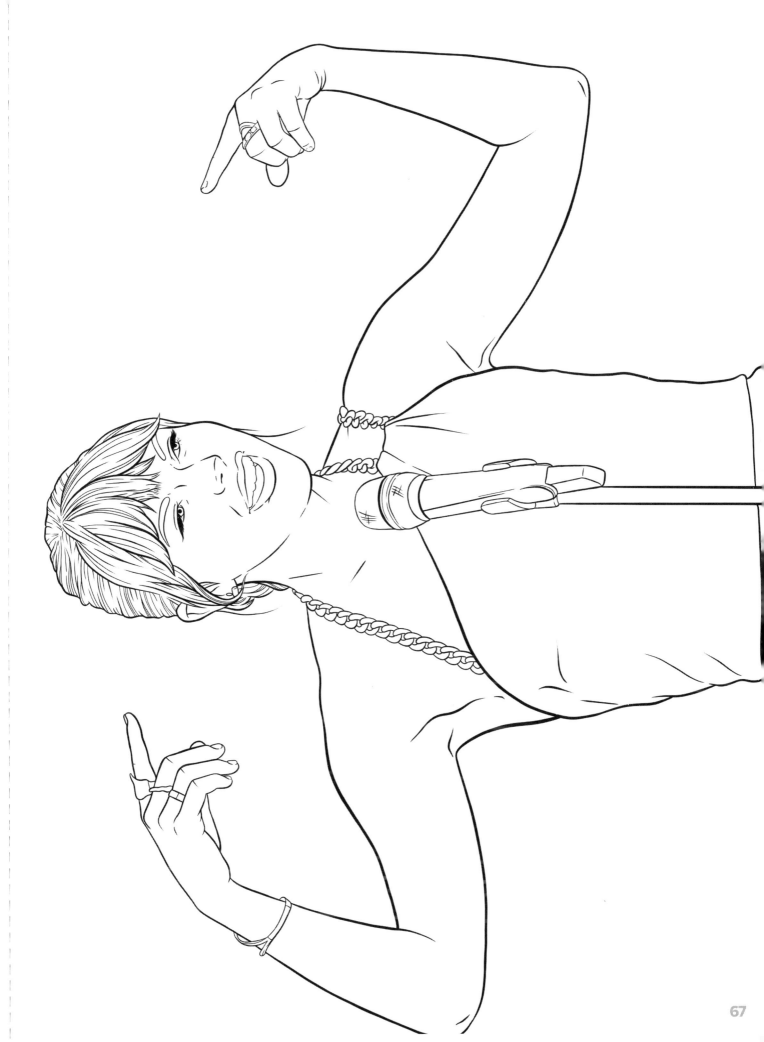

Woman of
the Decade

In 2019, Taylor became the first ever recipient of
Billboard's Woman of the Decade award. She was
given the title in recognition of her incredible musical
accomplishments, as well as her charity and activism.

Birthday Surprise!

While performing at a concert
on her 30th birthday, Taylor was surprised
on stage with a huge cake—decorated with
pictures of her cats, of course!

Tyler Swift

The music video for "The Man" focuses on the character of Tyler Swift—Taylor's male alter ego—and explores sexism and double standards faced by women. The end of the video reveals that Tyler is actually played by Taylor herself, under lots of clever prosthetics and makeup!

Flower Power

At the Grammy Awards in 2021, Taylor wore a beautiful dress covered in flowers. As the COVID-19 pandemic was ongoing, she also had a matching face mask—who says you can't be safe *and* stylish?

Con-graduations!

In May 2022, Taylor received an honorary doctorate from New York University. She attended that year's graduation ceremony and gave an inspirational speech to the students.

Sleepless Nights

Taylor said that her 10th album, *Midnights,* was "a collection of music written in the middle of the night." The electro-pop record is one of her most personal, exploring Taylor's anxieties and insecurities.

Super Songwriter

Taylor's clever lyrics and storytelling abilities are what make her music so unique and fascinating. Her songwriting skills even earned her the Songwriter-Artist of the Decade Award at the Nashville Songwriter Awards in 2022.

Grammy Glamour

In 2023, Taylor won the Grammy Award for Best Music Video for "All Too Well: The Short Film," which she wrote and directed herself. It was based on the epic 10-minute extended version of the song from *Red (Taylor's Version)*.

The Eras Tour

Taylor's long-awaited 2023 tour is a celebration of all the different musical styles used throughout her career. The spectacular show is over three hours long, featuring 44 songs from all of her albums.

Mazes

Taylor has lost her cats! Help her navigate the labyrinth to find them.

In 2019–2020, Taylor's masters (the original sound recordings of a song) were sold. In 2021, Taylor began rerecording all her music, releasing them as her own— Taylor's Version.

Help Taylor reclaim her name!

Word Search

Can you find nine of Taylor's studio album titles in the puzzle?

Albums

```
Y  Z  Q  D  M  A  D  F  Z  P  Y  B  F  T  L
Y  G  P  W  A  R  M  I  S  A  N  V  C  F  R
P  V  K  C  P  F  X  M  M  I  L  G  W  I  R
K  R  A  C  E  R  O  M  R  E  V  E  F  W  R
Y  A  Z  M  I  D  N  I  G  H  T  S  O  S  E
P  Z  S  J  L  J  G  C  P  F  S  L  L  R  P
T  O  Y  Q  J  I  R  X  H  E  P  J  K  O  U
W  W  W  U  Z  P  D  E  R  A  T  N  L  L  T
L  F  O  H  A  O  K  D  R  R  Y  L  O  Y  A
Y  A  L  N  D  C  V  Q  Z  L  B  E  R  A  T
C  J  C  R  K  K  A  L  S  E  J  C  E  T  I
P  H  W  S  E  A  J  N  E  S  B  X  Z  Q  O
C  K  E  L  O  V  E  R  E  S  D  H  B  K  N
V  Y  E  V  A  Y  S  P  F  K  B  T  J  F  P
W  J  G  B  V  M  T  F  S  E  C  R  K  P  S
```

Find these words...

TAYLOR SWIFT	RED	FOLKLORE
FEARLESS	REPUTATION	EVERMORE
SPEAK NOW	LOVER	MIDNIGHTS

Word Search

Find the names of Taylor's hit songs
hidden in this word search!

Hit Songs

```
I  F  P  W  Y  V  S  P  W  T  W  R  R  N  M
T  E  F  N  O  B  J  R  S  T  Y  D  E  A  B
L  W  E  O  B  B  J  T  J  Z  Q  F  D  A  V
L  T  O  E  T  N  Z  C  E  X  J  F  S  Q  X
E  N  H  L  V  I  T  O  R  E  H  I  T  N  A
W  N  A  E  L  C  E  M  P  U  W  Y  E  L  L
O  K  B  G  M  I  W  K  Z  J  Q  U  O  K  D
O  Y  C  V  I  A  W  Z  A  G  T  V  M  R  R
T  X  U  J  Y  D  N  R  G  H  E  T  I  B  O
L  V  Q  T  Z  C  R  D  R  S  S  U  N  M  U
L  X  G  R  O  S  G  A  T  C  R  O  E  F  R
A  O  H  F  J  K  V  O  C  D  K  Z  F  W  T
T  M  I  C  T  I  R  O  F  Y  D  A  E  R  G
W  B  U  D  M  Y  U  F  G  R  I  U  O  G  H
W  W  A  R  G  C  M  M  I  T  H  J  O  L  Y
```

Find these words...

MINE	TIM MCGRAW	READY FOR IT	WILLOW
RED	LOVE STORY	THE MAN	ALL TOO WELL
	SHAKE IT OFF	CARDIGAN	ANTI-HERO

Word Search

Can you find all the Taylor-themed
words hidden below?

Taylor Terms

Y	T	V	J	N	U	M	O	D	B	S	X	Z	X	M
O	S	A	P	D	Q	N	I	M	A	J	N	E	B	E
L	A	T	Y	K	E	W	G	K	Q	H	I	P	Q	A
I	R	D	Z	L	Q	I	R	R	T	X	O	Q	P	O
V	E	X	T	B	O	C	R	J	Y	Z	R	E	F	E
I	T	L	H	A	X	R	B	U	J	M	D	J	E	C
A	S	S	I	O	H	W	S	I	P	R	H	O	I	O
H	Y	F	R	B	N	Y	H	V	I	J	J	L	T	B
T	N	Y	T	B	O	N	U	Y	E	R	Y	K	F	E
I	H	B	E	Q	C	T	P	Z	G	R	U	E	I	D
D	T	X	E	D	I	S	U	A	I	G	S	T	W	L
E	I	A	N	I	S	K	F	C	F	J	L	I	S	G
R	B	A	N	N	V	L	S	Z	F	N	L	R	O	U
E	A	U	R	G	G	E	R	E	T	S	A	E	N	N
M	R	E	D	X	S	S	T	Q	B	F	R	X	T	G

Find these words...

TAYLOR'S VERSION	THIRTEEN	ICON	BENJAMIN
EASTER EGG	LYRICS	OLIVIA	
ERAS	SWIFTIE	MEREDITH	

Word Search

Find all the friendship bracelet
sayings in the letters below!

Friendship Bracelets

```
C N O I T A T U P E R G I B H
I K W B J U R D L J S A U A C
S E I F A N C Y O U M T T H G
S E N A I X H E A Y Z E E H T
A U V U Q O G A Q U R E F A Q
L J E A C V N H E S R W C U H
C D I C E Q T W G C M A J I U
P L T L P L L O A R S E H H Z
I M F J Z D N P V I P P Q E H
L Y I S K N T M A E T V G M T
D X W O A A P M U C M D V S V
E Q S H I Q R F U T J N H T T
R V A N O A I U M W U I Y I M
N T I L K E N D L P B A P Z H
E E T E I L U J E M Y R R A M
```

Find these words...

AUTUMN LEAVES	HATERS GONNA HATE	KARMA IS A CAT	SWIFTIE
BIG REPUTATION	I FANCY YOU	MARRY ME JULIET	
CHEER CAPTAIN	IT'S ME HI	RED LIP CLASSIC	

Quiz

Easy

1. What is Taylor's middle name?
   - [ ] Alison
   - [ ] Betty
   - [ ] Marjorie
   - [ ] Dorothea

2. What was the title of her debut album?

   _____

3. What year was she born?

   _____

4. Complete the lyric:
   "It's a love story, baby,

   _____ "

5. What is Taylor's
   lucky number?

   _____

6. Which of her albums was the first to be rerecorded as "Taylor's Version"?

   _____

7. Which of these instruments can Taylor play?
   - [ ] Guitar
   - [ ] Piano
   - [ ] Banjo
   - [ ] All of the above

8. What is the name of her 2023 tour?

   _____

9. Which US state did Taylor move to as a teenager to pursue her music career?

   _____

10. Taylor has won over 500 awards during her career.
    - [ ] True
    - [ ] False

Quiz
Medium

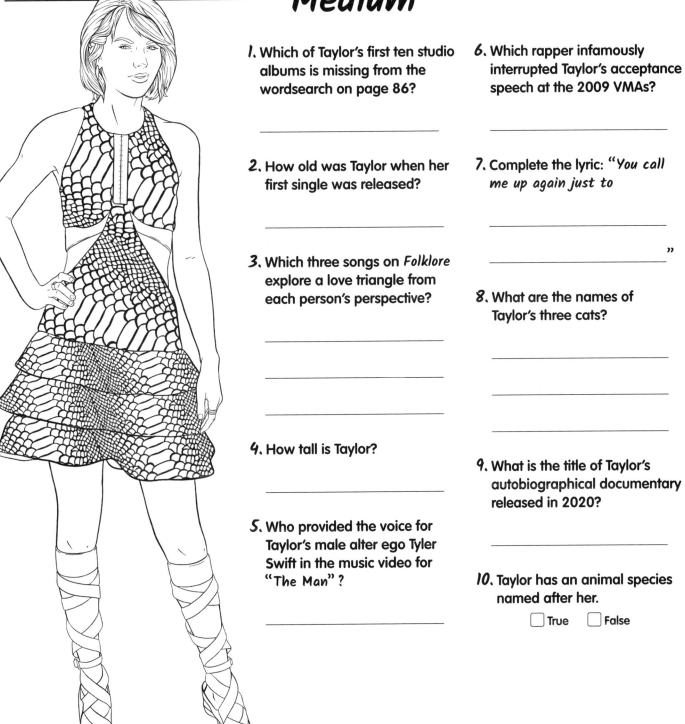

1. Which of Taylor's first ten studio albums is missing from the wordsearch on page 86?

_____

2. How old was Taylor when her first single was released?

_____

3. Which three songs on *Folklore* explore a love triangle from each person's perspective?

_____

_____

_____

4. How tall is Taylor?

_____

5. Who provided the voice for Taylor's male alter ego Tyler Swift in the music video for "The Man"?

_____

6. Which rapper infamously interrupted Taylor's acceptance speech at the 2009 VMAs?

_____

7. Complete the lyric: "*You call me up again just to*

_____

_____ "

8. What are the names of Taylor's three cats?

_____

_____

_____

9. What is the title of Taylor's autobiographical documentary released in 2020?

_____

10. Taylor has an animal species named after her.

☐ True   ☐ False

Quiz
Hard

1. What was Taylor's first number one single on the Billboard Hot 100?

   _____

2. In 2019, Taylor broke the Guinness World Record (previously held by Michael Jackson) for winning the most of which award?

   _____

3. Which singer was Taylor named after?

   _____

4. Complete the lyric: "*Did you hear my covert narcissism,*

   _____

   _____ "

5. What Swedish pseudonym (fake name) has Taylor previously used as a songwriter?

   _____

6. Joe Alwyn also co-wrote songs under a fake name on *Folklore* and *Evermore*, what was it?

   _____

7. Who did Taylor duet with on the track "*The Last Time*"?

   _____

8. In 2021, Taylor wrote and directed the short film "*All Too Well*" based on her song of the same name. Which actors starred in the two lead roles?

   _____

   _____

9. What was the name of the contest-winning poem that Taylor wrote when she was 10?
   - [ ] Pen in My Hand
   - [ ] Monster in My Closet
   - [ ] Pebble in My Shoe
   - [ ] Gum in My Hair

10. Who can be heard at the very beginning of "*Gorgeous*"?

   _____

Word Scramble

Unscramble Taylor's Albums!

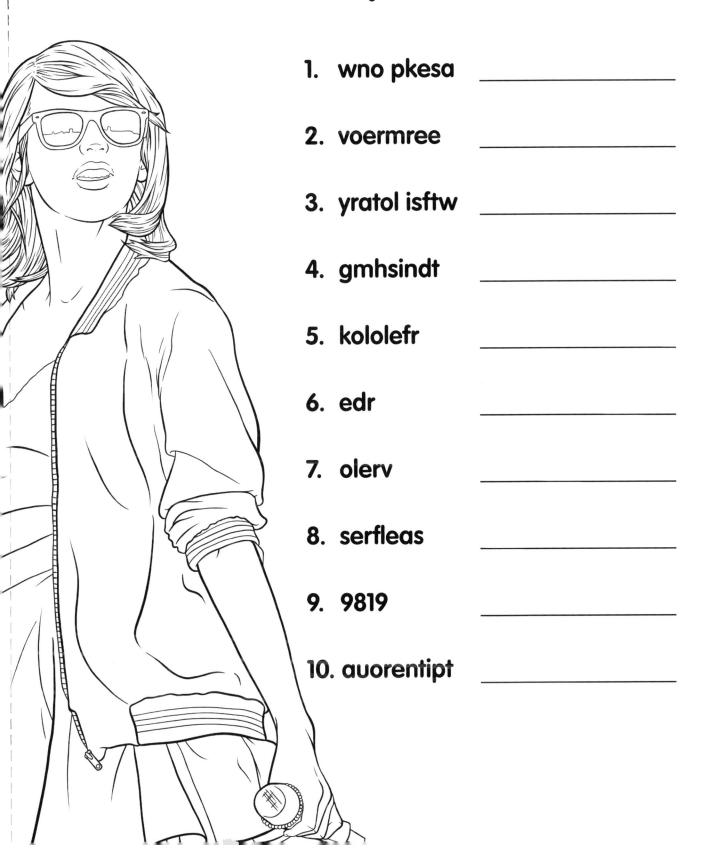

1. wno pkesa _____

2. voermree _____

3. yratol isftw _____

4. gmhsindt _____

5. kololefr _____

6. edr _____

7. olerv _____

8. serfleas _____

9. 9819 _____

10. auorentipt _____

Mazes

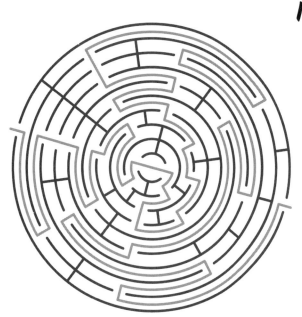

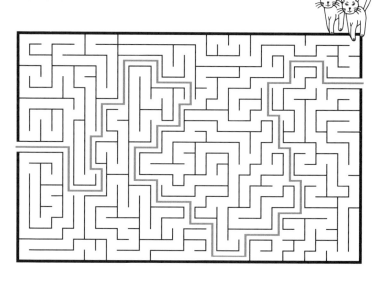

Spot the Difference

Word Searches

Albums

```
Y Z Q D M A D F Z P Y B F T L
Y G P W A R M I S A N V C F R
P V K C P F X M M I L G W I R
K R A C E R O M R E V E F W R
Y A Z M I D N I G H T S O S E
P Z S J L J G C P F S L L R R
T O Y Q J I R X H E P J K O U
W W W U Z P D E R A T N L L T
L F O H A O K D R R Y L O Y A
Y A L N D C V Q Z L B E R A T
C J C R K K A L S E J C E T I
P H W S E A J N E S B X Z Q O
C K E L O V E R E S D H B K N
V Y E V A Y S P F K B T J F P
W J G B V M T F S E C R K P S
```

Hit Songs

```
I F P W Y V S P W T W R R N M
T E F N O B J R S T Y D E A B
L W E O B B J T J Z Q F D A V
L T O E T N Z C E X J F S Q X
E N H L V I T O R E H I T N A
W N A E L C E M P U W Y E L L
O K B G M I W K Z J Q U O K D
O Y C V I A W Z A G T V M R R
T X U J Y D N R G H E T I B O
L V Q T Z C R D R S S U N M U
L X G R O S G A T C R O E F R
A O H F J K V O C D K Z F W T
T M I C T I R O F Y D A E R G
W B U D M Y U F G R I U O G H
W W A R G C M M I T H J O L Y
```

Taylor Terms

```
Y T V J N U M O D B S X Z X M
O S A P D Q N I M A J N E B E
L A T Y K E W G K Q H I P Q A
I R D Z L Q I R R T X O Q P A
V E X T B O C R J Y Z R E F E
I T L H A X R B U J M D J E C
A S S I O H W S I P R H O I O
H Y F R B N Y H V I J J L T B
T N Y T B O N U Y E R Y K F E
I H B E Q C T P Z G R U E I D
D T X E D I S U A I G S T W L
E I A N I S K F C F J L I S G
R B A N N V L S Z F N L R O U
E A U R G G E R E T S A E N N
M R E D X S S T Q B F R X T G
```

Friendship Bracelets

```
C N O I T A T U P E R G I B H
I K W B J U R D L J S A U A C
S E I F A N C Y O U M T T H G
S E N A I X H E A Y Z E E H T
A U V U Q O G A Q U R E F A Q
L J E A C V N H E S R W C U H
C D I C E Q T W G C M A J I U
P L T L P L L O A R S E H H Z
I M F J Z D N P V I P P Q E H
L Y I S K N T M A E T V G M T
D X W O A A P M U C M D V S V
E Q S H I Q R F U T J N H T T
R V A N O A I U M W U I Y I M
N T I L K E N D L P B A P Z H
E E T E I L U J E M Y R R A M
```

ANSWER KEY

Quizzes

Easy
1. Alison
2. *Taylor Swift*
3. 1989
4. "Just say yes," from "Love Story"
5. 13
6. *Fearless*
7. All of the above
8. The Eras Tour
9. Tennessee
10. True

Medium
1. 1989
2. 16
3. "Cardigan," "August," and "Betty"
4. About 5ft 10in, or 1.78m
5. Dwayne Johnson
6. Kanye West
7. "Break me like a promise," from "All Too Well"
8. Meredith Grey, Olivia Benson, and Benjamin Button
9. *Miss Americana*
10. True—a millipede called *Nannaria swiftae*

Hard
1. "We Are Never Ever Getting Back Together"
2. American Music Award (AMA)
3. James Taylor
4. "I disguise as altruism," from "Anti-Hero"
5. Nils Sjöberg
6. William Bowery
7. Gary Lightbody
8. Sadie Sink & Dylan O'Brien
9. Monster in My Closet
10. James Reynolds—the daughter of Blake Lively & Ryan Reynolds

Word Scramble
1. speak now
2. evermore
3. taylor swift
4. midnights
5. folklore
6. red
7. lover
8. fearless
9. 1989
10. reputation